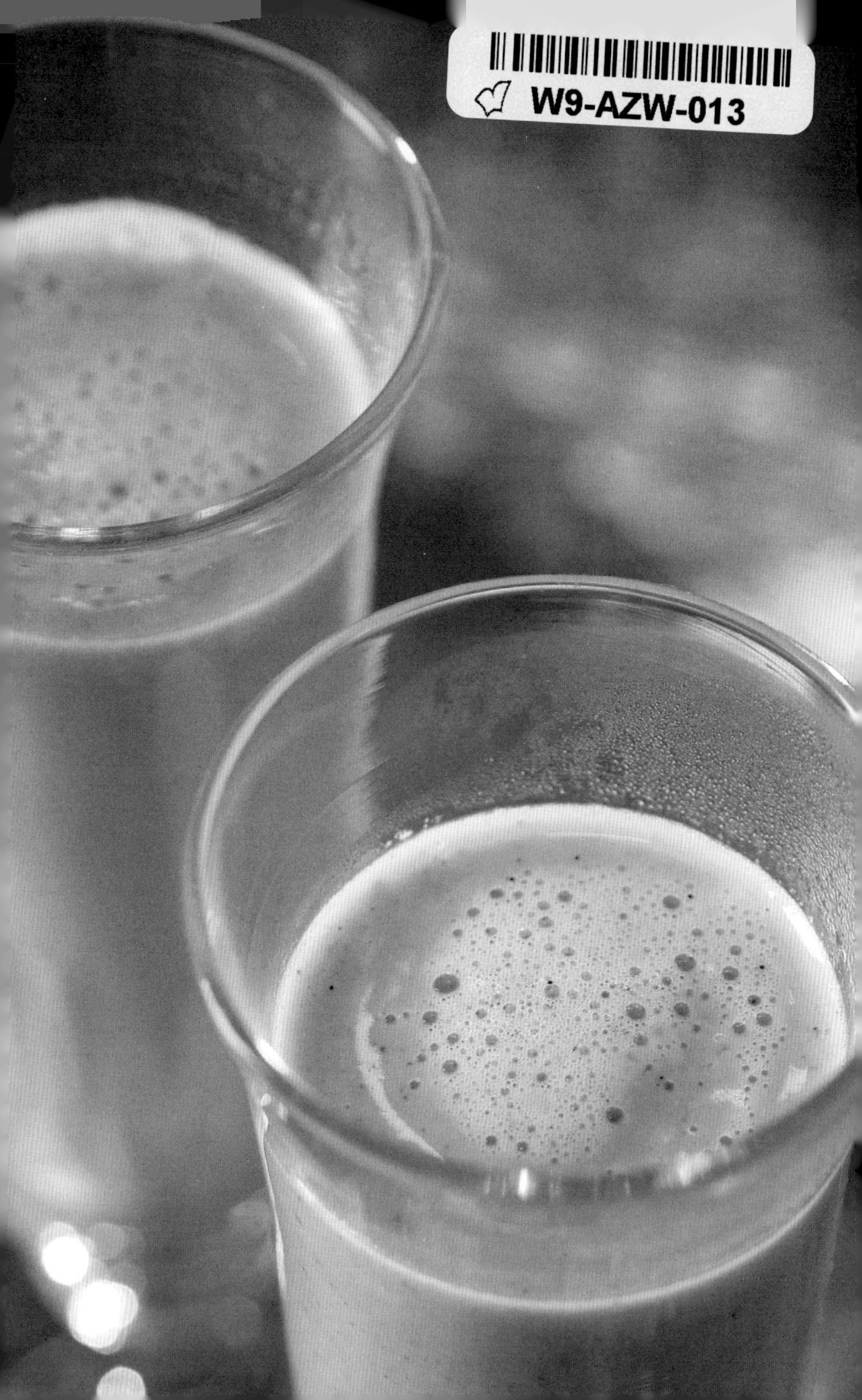

HOT *Drinks*

HOT *Drinks*

over 25 warming recipes for cold days

RYLAND PETERS & SMALL
LONDON • NEW YORK

Senior designer Toni Kay
Picture manager Christina Borsi
Production controller Mai-Ling Collyer
Art director Leslie Harrington
Editorial director Julia Charles
Publisher Cindy Richards
Indexer Vanessa Bird

First published in 2017 by
Ryland Peters & Small
20–21 Jockey's Fields, London WC1R 4BW
and
341 E 116th St, New York NY 10029
www.rylandpeters.com

10 9 8 7 6 5 4 3 2 1

Text copyright © Tonia George, Hannah Miles,
Louise Pickford, Ben Reed, Will Torrent and
Ryland Peters & Small 2017

Design and photographs copyright ©
Ryland Peters & Small 2017

ISBN: 978-1-84975-896-3

Printed in China

A CIP record for this book is available from
the British Library.

US Library of Congress Cataloging-in-Publication Data
has been applied for.

NOTES
• All spoon measurements are level unless otherwise
stated.
• All eggs are medium, unless otherwise specified. It is
generally recommended that free-range eggs be used.
Recipes containing raw or partially cooked egg should
not be served to the very young, very old, anyone with
a compromised immune system or pregnant women.

CONTENTS

SOME LIKE IT HOT...

For many of us around the world, a hot drink is a daily ritual. Whether this is morning coffee, afternoon tea or a milky nightcap, it has become ingrained in our lives, perhaps more than any other food or beverage. Whilst both tea and coffee in all their various forms are the most widely consumed hot drinks, there is a huge variety of other beverages to prepare and serve warm or hot, either alcoholic versions, such as mulled wines, or milky drinks infused with herbs, spices and aromatics.

This book is a collection of flavoured coffees, hot chocolates, alcoholic drinks and milky concoctions guaranteed to stimulate mind, body or soul – often all three at once. As many are stimulants, their appeal is instantly recognizable. But it is not just the satisfaction we gain physically from these drinks that makes them so attractive – there is often an emotional and nostalgic attachment stemming from childhood or festive occasions when many drinks come into their own.

We often associate hot drinks with colder climates, yet culturally and historically this isn't necessarily so. For sure, many of the mulled spiced wines such as Glühwein (or glow wine) originate from Germany and other eastern European and Scandinavian countries where getting warm quickly is essential during the bitterly cold winter months. However, the majority of hot drinks hail from warm climes. Coffee was first discovered in Ethiopia and quickly travelled to the Middle East, chocolate (or cocoa) was cultivated as far back as 1000 BC by the Mayans and Aztecs in Mexico, and the tea ceremonies of China and Japan are likewise steeped in a fascinating history, with cultivation of tea dating back to 1100 BC.

The benefits of consuming hot drinks are many, yet their greatest appeal can be the pleasure derived not only from the drinking but often from the process of gently warming and stirring various combinations until they almost boil. With so many wonderful hot drinks to choose from in this book, you should find something delicious to drink on any occasion throughout the year.

The book is divided into chapters determined by the main ingredient of each recipe. For all chocoholics out there, the first chapter on Hot Chocolates contains a fabulous selection of rich and comforting hot chocolate drinks inspired by beverages from around the globe,

including Aztec Hot Chocolate with a hidden kick from the addition of chilli, Minted Hot Chocolate with a refreshing hint of mint, and a classic winter warmer, Gingerbread Hot Chocolate.

The chapter on Milky Drinks is bound to be a hit with all the family as it includes plenty of delicious milk drinks that kids will love. The Turkish Delight Frothy is a pretty, delicate drink, while Peanut Butter Crunch is a wickedly sweet and indulgent treat for children and grown-ups alike and Malted Milk makes a soothing bedtime drink.

The chapter on Coffees includes several timeless classics from around the world, including Turkish Coffee and Thai Coffee, as well as some more unusual and innovative drinks such as Pumpkin Latte and Mocha Maple Coffee. Coffee and rum make perfect partners, so in this chapter you will also find recipes for Caribbean Café with Rum and Malibu and a Catalan Coffee Punch.

As the days get shorter and the chill of winter starts to bite, what could be more inviting than the idea of sipping warmed Toddies and Mulls in front of a roaring fire? Although many of the mulled drinks tend to be associated with Christmas, such as thanks to their earthy spices and festive flavours, there are many others that have no such seasonal restrictions – try a Hot Buttered Rum or a Portuguese Mulled Port. The healing properties of a Hot Tea Toddy will help ward off a cold any time of the year, while a Mulled Bloody Mary is the perfect answer if you have over-indulged the night before!

Hot Chocolates

HOT CHOCOLATE WITH CHILLI

Use the best quality cocoa powder you can find. The heat of the chilli/chile takes this chocolate drink to another dimension!

2 teaspoons unsweetened cocoa powder

600 ml/2½ cups whole milk, or 300 ml/1¼ cups milk mixed with 300 ml/1¼ cups single/light cream

1 teaspoon chopped dried chilli/chile or ½ teaspoon chopped fresh red chilli/chile

sugar, to taste (optional)

Serves 2

Put the cocoa powder in a heatproof bowl, add about 1 tablespoon of the milk and mix to a smooth paste with a wooden spoon.

Put the remaining milk or milk and cream mixture in a saucepan, add the chilli/chile and bring to the boil. Carefully strain the boiling milk onto the cocoa paste through a fine-mesh sieve/strainer, then whisk vigorously.

Pour into two cups. Let cool for about 1 minute, then taste – you may need to add sugar. Serve immediately.

MALTED HOT CHOCOLATE

Malted drinks are some of the most comforting and this hot chocolate is just the thing to drink when you're in need of a hug in a mug. Include lots of malt powder, so that the hot chocolate is thick and syrupy, although you can add a little less if you prefer thinner hot chocolate. Top with whipped cream and malted chocolate balls for an extra-special treat.

100 g/3½ oz. milk chocolate, chopped

250 ml/1 cup milk

450 ml/1¾ cups double/ heavy cream

3 tablespoons malted drink powder (such as Horlicks or Ovaltine)

chocolate malt balls (such as Maltesers or Whoppers), chopped

Serves 2

Place the chopped chocolate in a heatproof bowl over a pan of simmering water and heat gently over a low heat until melted.

Place the milk and 250 ml/ 1 cup of the cream in a saucepan and bring gently to the boil. Add the melted chocolate to the pan with the malted drink powder and simmer over a low heat until the chocolate is combined, whisking all the time. Pour the hot chocolate into two cups.

Whip the remaining cream to stiff peaks and place a large spoonful on top of each drink. Sprinkle with the chopped malt balls and serve straight away.

MINTED HOT CHOCOLATE

Chocolate with a hint of after-dinner mints – just the thing to send you off into a peaceful sleep, or warm you up on a chilly winter's afternoon.

600 ml/2 cups milk

4 sprigs of fresh mint, bruised lightly to extract flavour

50 g/2 oz. dark/bittersweet chocolate (at least 70% cocoa solids), chopped

sugar, to taste (optional)

Serves 2

Put the milk and mint sprigs in a saucepan and heat very gently until boiling. Boil for 1 minute, then remove from the heat. Discard the mint.

Divide the chocolate between two cups. Pour in the hot milk and stir until the chocolate has melted. Serve the sugar separately, if using.

GINGERBREAD HOT CHOCOLATE

When you're sitting out in the cold around a fire, wrapped in sweaters, this is the perfect warmer. It's lovely with a dash of brandy... for the adults only, of course!

1 litre/4 cups whole milk

3 tablespoons ginger or gingerbread syrup

1 cinnamon stick

2 whole cloves

2–3 strips of orange peel

2 tablespoons brandy or orange-flavoured liqueur (optional)

450 g/3¾ cups dark/bittersweet chocolate, chopped

whipped cream and ground cinnamon, to serve (optional)

Serves 4-6

Pour the milk into a saucepan set over a medium heat. Add the ginger syrup, cinnamon stick, cloves, orange peel and brandy (if using) and bring slowly to the boil, stirring occasionally to allow the spices to infuse with the milk.

Meanwhile, tip the chopped chocolate into a large jug/pitcher. Pour the hot, spice-infused milk onto the chocolate and whisk until silky smooth. Strain into cups, top with whipped cream and dust with cinnamon, if using, and serve.

AZTEC HOT CHOCOLATE

Cacao was discovered by the Aztecs and was often referred to as the 'food of the gods' because of its richness and health benefits. The cacao was ground in a type of pestle and mortar with chilli/chile and other spices and hot water was added to make a drink. You can use normal chilli/chile powder, but for something more smoky, use a chipotle chilli/chile powder.

500 ml/2 cups cold water

2 tablespoons light brown sugar, clear honey or agave syrup

1 cinnamon stick

1 teaspoon pure vanilla extract or 1/2 vanilla pod/bean

3 cardamom pods, lightly bruised

1 strip of orange peel

1/2–1 teaspoon chilli/chile powder

a pinch of freshly grated nutmeg

200 g/1 1/2 cups dark/bittersweet chocolate (at least 70% cocoa solids), finely chopped

ground cinnamon, to serve

Serves 4

Pour the water into a saucepan set over a low heat. Add the sugar, cinnamon stick, vanilla, cardamom pods, orange peel, chilli/chile powder and nutmeg. Bring to a gentle simmer, then remove from the heat and set aside for 30 minutes to allow the spices to fully infuse with the water.

Discard the whole spices and orange peel. Add the chopped chocolate to the pan and reheat to just below boiling point, stirring constantly to smoothly melt the chocolate. If you wish, whizz the hot chocolate using a handheld mixer to ensure the hot chocolate is silky smooth and has a good foam on top.

Pour the hot chocolate into cups or heatproof glasses and serve immediately with a pinch of ground cinnamon on top.

CHOCOLATE MULLED WINE

This is the most decadent hot chocolate you will ever have, and the most indulgent mulled wine at the same time. A really fruity chocolate from the Dominican Republic, where the cocoa has a natural red fruit undertone to it, works really well with the richness of the red wine, port and spices. This is a great drink to serve at a Christmas party!

750 ml/3 cups red wine

2 cinnamon sticks

6 cloves

2 star anise

1 large sprig of fresh rosemary

2 bay leaves

4 cardamom pods

½ vanilla pod/bean

1 orange, sliced

200 g/1 cup soft light brown sugar

250 g/2 cups fruity dark/ bittersweet chocolate (such as Saint-Domingue from Cacao Barry), chopped

2 tablespoons ruby port (optional)

Serves 4–6

Pour the red wine into a saucepan set over a low heat. Add the cinnamon sticks, cloves, star anise, rosemary and bay leaves.

Lightly bruise the cardamom pods and add them to the pan, along with the half a vanilla pod/bean and the orange slices. Add the sugar and slowly heat the wine, taking care not to let it boil.

Remove the pan from the heat and set aside for 30 minutes to allow the spices to fully infuse with the wine.

Add the chopped chocolate to the pan and reheat to just below boiling point, stirring constantly to smoothly melt the chocolate. Add the port (if using), mix again and strain into heatproof glasses to serve.

Milky Drinks

MALTED MILK

There are several popular brands of malted milk available, but it is easy enough to make your own healthy version of this soothing bedtime drink.

500 ml/2 cups milk

3 tablespoons barley malt extract

freshly grated nutmeg, to serve

Serves 2

Put the milk and malt extract in a saucepan and heat gently until it just reaches boiling point. Whisk the milk with a balloon whisk until frothy, then pour it into two cups. Grate over a little nutmeg and serve.

TURKISH DELIGHT FROTHY

You can use any flavour Turkish delight you like in this pretty, delicate drink. The best bit is finding half-melted pieces of the Turkish delight at the bottom of the cup! Serve with a spoon.

500 ml/2 cups milk

50 g/2 oz. Turkish delight, cut into cubes, plus extra to top

125 ml/½ cup whipping cream

2 teaspoons rosewater

½ teaspoon honey

a pinch of ground cardamom

unsalted pistachio nuts, finely chopped, to serve

Serves 2

Put the milk and Turkish delight in a saucepan and heat gently, stirring constantly, until the mixture just reaches boiling point. Meanwhile, whip the cream, rosewater, honey and ground cardamom in a bowl until just stiff.

Pour the milk into two cups and top with the cream. Sprinkle with pieces of Turkish delight and pistachio nuts and serve immediately.

SAFFRON MILK

This drink is aromatic and exotic. The saffron, with its earthy flavour and striking colour, is pretty as well as delicious. The condensed milk does make this drink very sweet so, if you prefer, reduce the amount used and increase the quantity of milk.

500 ml/2 cups milk

60 ml/¼ cup sweetened condensed milk

¼ teaspoon saffron threads, plus extra to serve

3 green cardamom pods, lightly crushed

Serves 2

Put the milk, condensed milk, saffron and cardamom pods in a saucepan and heat gently, stirring constantly, until the mixture just reaches boiling point. Remove from the heat and set aside for 5 minutes to allow the milk to infuse.

Strain the milk into two heatproof glasses, sprinkle with a few saffron threads and serve immediately.

HONEY BABA

This is a delicately spiced milk drink infused with
a hint of honey. You can always add a little rum
to this for a grown-up version.

500 ml/2 cups milk

2 cinnamon sticks,
   lightly crushed

2 teaspoons honey

cinnamon sugar, to dust

Serves 2

Put the milk and cinnamon
sticks in a saucepan and heat
gently until the mixture just
reaches boiling point. Remove
from the heat and strain.

Add 1 teaspoon honey to each
cup and pour in the cinnamon-
infused milk. Dust with a little
cinnamon sugar and serve
immediately.

SPICED CHILLI COCONUT MILK

Coconut milk adds both a delicate flavour and a wonderful creaminess to this spiced drink. The slight hint of chilli/chile is exotic and warming.

250 ml/1 cup milk

250 ml/1 cup coconut milk

1½ tablespoons soft brown sugar

2 star anise, lightly crushed

1 small red chilli/chile, halved lengthways and deseeded

125 ml/½ cup double/heavy cream

toasted shredded coconut, to serve

Serves 2

Put all the ingredients, except the double/heavy cream and toasted coconut, in a saucepan. Heat gently for 10 minutes, then bring just to boiling point. Strain into two cups.

Whip the cream until it holds its shape and spoon over the drinks. Sprinkle with a little toasted coconut to serve.

PEANUT BUTTER CRUNCH

A big hit with the kids (and also with grown-up lovers of peanut butter!), this is a deliciously creamy, nutty drink.

500 ml/2 cups milk

3 tablespoons crunchy/natural peanut butter

1 tablespoon maple syrup

60 ml/¼ cup whipping cream

ground cinnamon, to serve

Serves 2

Put the milk, peanut butter and maple syrup in a saucepan and heat gently, stirring constantly, until it just reaches boiling point and the peanut butter has melted. Froth the mixture using a balloon whisk.

Divide between two heatproof glasses or cups. Whip the cream until it holds its shape and spoon over the drinks. Dust with a little cinnamon to serve.

CHRISTMAS MILK

A mince pie in a mug – yummy. The star decoration on top
is fun, but optional – the drink tastes great either way!

1 litre/4 cups milk

4 tablespoons raisins

2 tablespoons chopped
crystallized ginger

4 teaspoons clear honey

½ an unwaxed orange, sliced

60 ml/¼ cup whipping cream

cinnamon sugar, to dust

*a piece of card and a star-
shaped pastry cutter, about
5 cm/2 inches in diameter*

Serves 4–6

Using the pastry cutter as a
template, carefully draw a star
on the card. Use scissors to cut
out the star shape to create a
stencil. Set aside until needed.

Put the milk, raisins, ginger,
honey and orange slices in a
saucepan. Heat gently until
it just reaches boiling point.
Strain the mixture and divide
between the cups. Lightly whip
the cream until foaming and
spoon it over the drinks.

Hold the stencil over each drink,
making sure that the star shape
is in the centre. Lightly dust
with cinnamon sugar and
remove the stencil to leave a
star decoration on the whipped
cream. Repeat with all the
drinks and serve immediately.

Coffee Drinks

....

THAI COFFEE

Coffee in Thailand is often served iced but can be served hot too. It is always very sweet as it is served over sweetened condensed milk. You can either stir the coffee and milk together or drink the hot coffee first and then enjoy the warm milk underneath.

160 ml/^{2}/$_3$ cup sweetened condensed milk, at room temperature

375 ml/1½ cups freshly brewed strong, hot coffee

Serves 2

Divide the condensed milk between two heatproof glasses, then very carefully pour in the coffee so that it sits on top of the milk. Stir if you like, then drink straight away.

Variation Add a little freshly ground cardamom and coriander to the ground coffee before brewing.

TURKISH COFFEE

When brewing Turkish coffee there are several important points to remember. You will need very finely ground coffee (or grind it yourself until it's finer than espresso coffee grains) and a small pot to heat the coffee and water together. Called a 'cezve', this is a small copper pot with a lip on one side and handle on the other (see photo). Never take your eyes off the heating process – if the mixture boils over, it makes quite a mess. In Turkey coffee is nearly always sweetened, but this is optional.

625 ml/2½ cups cold water

2 teaspoons extra-finely ground coffee

sugar, to taste (optional)

Serves 2

Put the water in a small saucepan (ideally a Turkish coffee pot, see above). Stir in the coffee and sugar, if using. Heat very gently until the coffee just reaches boiling point.

Pour enough coffee into two small coffee cups to come about halfway up, then reheat the remaining coffee until it almost boils again. Add the remaining coffee to the cups and let stand for 1 minute before drinking. Sweeten with sugar if you wish.

MOCHA MAPLE COFFEE

Coffee and chocolate make perfect partners, as this delicious drink proves. The addition of sweet, maple-flavoured cream makes this an indulgent treat and the perfect after-dinner drink.

500 ml/2 cups freshly brewed hot coffee

2 shots crème de cacao or chocolate syrup

125 ml/½ cup whipping cream

1 teaspoon maple syrup

grated dark/bittersweet chocolate, to sprinkle

Serves 2

Pour the freshly brewed coffee into two heatproof glasses and add a shot of crème de cacao or chocolate syrup to each one.

Lightly whisk the cream and maple syrup together until the mixture is foaming and thickened slightly. Slowly layer the cream over the surface of the coffee using a flat-bottomed barspoon or a teaspoon. Sprinkle with grated chocolate and serve immediately.

VANILLA COFFEE

Grinding freshly roasted coffee beans with chopped vanilla pods/beans produces a lovely, naturally flavoured coffee with just the right aroma and taste. Once ground, use at once or keep in a screw-top jar until ready to use.

25 g/1 oz. coffee beans

2 vanilla pods/beans, roughly chopped

milk and sugar, to taste (optional)

Serves 4

Put the coffee beans and vanilla pods/beans in a coffee grinder and grind finely. Use this mixture to make coffee in your preferred method, adding milk and/or sugar if you wish.

CATALAN COFFEE PUNCH

This is a traditional hot coffee and rum drink from the Catalonia region of Spain. The alcohol is burnt off before the coffee is added. It is traditional to use a terracotta cooking vessel for this, but a stainless-steel saucepan will work just as well. Be careful when igniting the rum, and use an extra-long match or a taper to keep your hands well away from the flame.

250 ml/1 cup white rum

1–2 tablespoons caster/
   superfine sugar

1 cinnamon stick

2 strips of unwaxed lemon zest

500 ml/2 cups freshly brewed
   hot coffee

Serves 6-8

Put the rum, sugar, cinnamon and lemon zest in a terracotta pot (or other flameproof dish) and carefully ignite the mixture.

Let the flame die down completely, then slowly pour in the hot coffee. Strain the mixture and divide between heavy-based shot glasses or heatproof demitasse cups and serve.

CARIBBEAN CAFE WITH RUM AND MALIBU

This exotic flavoured coffee is similar to an Irish coffee where the alcohol and coffee are combined in a glass, then lightly whipped cream is carefully poured on top over the back of a spoon so it floats on the surface. Traditionally you then drink the coffee through the layer of frothy cream.

2–4 teaspoons sugar, to taste

2 tablespoons dark rum

2 tablespoons Malibu

250 ml/1 cup freshly brewed hot coffee

80 ml/⅓ cup whipping cream

Serves 2

Divide the sugar, rum, Malibu and coffee between two heatproof glasses and stir well.

Put the cream in a bowl and whisk until foaming. Slowly layer the cream over the surface of each coffee, using a flat-bottomed barspoon or a teaspoon. Serve immediately.

PUMPKIN LATTE

Perfect for Halloween, this thick, richly spiced latte is flavoured with sweetened pumpkin. If you can find canned sweetened pumpkin purée, then use this and omit the sugar in the recipe.

375 ml/1½ cups milk

100 g/3½ oz. cooked sweet pumpkin, mashed, or canned pumpkin purée

3 tablespoons brown sugar (omit if using canned purée)

¼ teaspoon ground cinnamon

250 ml/1 cup freshly brewed hot coffee

whipped cream and cinnamon sugar, to serve

Serves 3

Put the milk, pumpkin, sugar (if using) and cinnamon in a saucepan and heat gently, whisking constantly until the mixture just reaches boiling point. Transfer to three cups or heatproof glasses and stir in the coffee.

Serve topped with lightly whipped cream and a dusting of cinnamon sugar.

EGG-NOG LATTE

This warming, festive drink with a hint of coffee makes
a lovely alternative to the more traditional egg nog.
For a non-alcoholic version, omit the rum.

500 ml/2 cups milk

1 vanilla pod/bean, split

2 very fresh eggs

2–3 tablespoons caster/superfine
   sugar, to taste

½ teaspoon ground cinnamon

a pinch of grated nutmeg

2 tablespoons dark rum

250 ml/1 cup freshly brewed
   hot coffee

Serves 4

Put the milk and vanilla pod/
bean in a saucepan and heat
gently until the milk just
reaches boiling point.

Meanwhile, put the eggs,
sugar and spices in a bowl and
whisk until frothy. Stir in the
milk, then return the mixture
to the pan. Heat gently for
2–3 minutes, stirring constantly
with a wooden spoon, until
the mixture thickens slightly.

Remove from the heat and stir
in the rum and coffee. Discard
the vanilla pod/bean. Pour
into four heatproof glasses
and serve immediately.

Toddies & Mulls

THE HOT TODDY

For some reason this drink is often only consumed when the drinker feels under the weather, but the hot toddy is perfect for sipping after any outdoor activity when the temperature has turned frosty.

50 ml/2 oz. Scotch whisky

1 tablespoon dark honey

25 ml/1 oz. fresh lemon juice

a pinch of ground cinnamon
   or 1 cinnamon stick

boiling water, to top up

2 pieces of lemon zest, studded
   with cloves, to garnish

Serves 1

Add all the ingredients to a heatproof glass and stir gently to mix. Top up with boiling water and serve garnished with a piece of lemon zest studded with cloves.

HOT BUTTERED RUM

Rum may be the perfect ingredient for a summer Caribbean-style cocktail, but it also happily lends itself to winter nights, with the sweetness of the rum combining with the spices and the brown sugar. Try also adding cinnamon or vanilla to the mix for added complexity.

1 tablespoon brown sugar

50 ml/2 oz. dark rum

½ teaspoon allspice

1 teaspoon butter

hot water, to top up

a piece of orange zest studded with cloves, to garnish

Serves 1

Warm a heat-resistant glass and add the sugar and a little hot water. Stir until the sugar has dissolved, then add the rum, allspice and butter. Top up with hot water and stir until the butter has melted. Garnish with a piece of orange zest studded with cloves and serve.

HOT TEA TODDY

A cure-all for colds as well as a good night-time drink to help you sleep. Try to use a subtle whisky, such as Scotch or a single malt, not bourbon or Tennessee, which are too strongly flavoured. The amount of lemon and honey is very much down to personal preference, so taste as you go.

2 lemons, plus extra juice to taste

6 cloves

2 camomile tea bags or 1 tablespoon camomile tea leaves

400 ml/1¾ cups just-boiled water

2 cinnamon sticks

a pinch of freshly grated nutmeg

1–3 tablespoons clear honey, plus extra to taste

90 ml/3 oz. whisky

Serves 2

Cut half a lemon into slices and stud the skin of each slice with the cloves. Put the tea bags, hot water, cinnamon, nutmeg and lemon slices in a saucepan and simmer for 2–3 minutes.

Meanwhile, squeeze the juice from the remaining lemons. Take the tea mixture off the heat and add the lemon juice, honey and whisky. Taste and add more lemon or honey if necessary.

Strain the tea into two heatproof glasses or mugs and drop a lemon slice and cinnamon stick into each glass. Give it one final stir with the cinnamon stick before drinking.

MULLED WINE

Traditionally made with red wine, sugar and spices, this drink is always served hot. Try not to let your mixture boil when you heat it as this may impair the flavour.

2 x 75 cl bottles red wine

100 ml/⅓ cup brandy

zest and freshly squeezed juice of 2 clementines

zest of 1 lime

zest of 1 lemon

200 g/1 cup caster/superfine sugar

1 cinnamon stick

4 cloves

4 pinches of grated nutmeg

1 vanilla pod/bean, split

lemon zest and cinnamon sticks, to garnish

Serves 10

Add all the ingredients to a large saucepan set over a medium heat. Simmer gently for about 30 minutes, stirring occasionally.

Serve in heatproof glasses garnished with extra lemon zest and cinnamon sticks.

MULLED BLOODY MARY

This tastes exactly as you'd imagine a warmed version of the classic brunch drink to be. It is perfect for a cold winter's morning, especially if you've over-indulged the night before!

1 litre/4 cups **tomato juice**

1 unwaxed **lemon**

1–2 tablespoons **Worcestershire sauce**, to taste

80–125 ml/3–4 oz. **vodka**

a pinch of **celery salt**

sea salt and freshly ground **black pepper**

Serves 4-6

Put the tomato juice in a saucepan. Cut half the lemon into slices and squeeze the juice from the remaining half into the pan. Add the lemon slices, Worcestershire sauce and salt and pepper to taste. Bring slowly to the boil and simmer gently, uncovered, for 10 minutes.

Remove the saucepan from the heat and let cool for about 15 minutes. Stir in the vodka and celery salt to taste. Serve in tall heatproof glasses.

HOT RUM AND CIDER PUNCH

The perfect autumnal drink with its slices of apple infused with the flavours of the cider, rum and spices, this would make a great drink for a Halloween party. If you want to serve a family–friendly, non-alcoholic version, replace the cider with apple juice and omit the rum.

500-ml bottle traditional dry cider/2 cups hard apple cider

2 slices of unwaxed lemon

1 apple, cored and thinly sliced

1 cinnamon stick, crushed

3 cloves

2 tablespoons soft light brown sugar

80 ml/3 oz. dark rum

Serves 4-6

Put the cider, lemon slices, apple slices, cinnamon, cloves, sugar and rum in a saucepan and heat the mixture gently until it just reaches boiling point. Simmer very gently for 10 minutes, then remove from the heat and let infuse for 10 minutes.

Ladle into small heatproof glasses or cups to serve.

PORTUGUESE MULLED PORT

Similar to mulled wine but made using port, this is an elegant spiced punch perfect for a winter cocktail party. It is fairly potent so serve it in small demitasse cups (or glasses) as an aperitif.

2 unwaxed oranges

500 ml/2 cups water

50 g/¼ cup brown sugar

10 cloves, lightly crushed

6 allspice berries, crushed

1 cinnamon stick, crushed

¼ teaspoon freshly grated nutmeg

75 cl bottle ruby port

Serves 12

Peel and slice one orange and squeeze the juice from the second orange. Put the slices and juice in a saucepan and add the water, sugar, cloves, allspice, cinnamon stick and nutmeg.

Bring slowly to the boil, stirring until the sugar is dissolved. Simmer gently for 10 minutes. Stir in the port and heat gently, without boiling, for a further 2–3 minutes.

Strain and pour into small cups or heatproof glasses to serve.

PHOTOGRAPHY CREDITS

RECIPE CREDITS

INDEX